Acorns to Great Oaks

Meditations for Children

by Marie Delanote

illustrations by Jokanies

FINDHORN PRESS

How To Use This Book

Every meditation in this book is linked to a specific emotion or goal a child might want to achieve. To start, have your child identify the issue they are struggling with by consulting the table of contents across this page and choosing the relevant exercise from the list.

Once your child has chosen their meditation, read the words out loud for them so they know what to expect, and let them have a good look at the illustrations. Each illustration is based on the words in the meditation, so your child can easily envision what they are supposed to "see" in their mind. Not every child finds this easy.

When your child is ready, have them sit or lie down and close their eyes. Make sure they know that there is no right or wrong way to do the meditation. Whatever they experience is okay! It is useful to practise particular meditations at times when they are not feeling sad or angry or experiencing certain emotions, as then they will understand what to do when they really need it. Allow them to play with this so they feel comfortable.

As a parent or carer, encourage your child to apply these coping mechanisms on a daily basis. For example, on the drive to school in the morning, you could ask your child which colour balloon they feel comfortable in today. When you see something happening on the road, encourage them to sprinkle fairy dust over the incident in order to help others, and so on. Make it a part of daily life. Have fun with it! We are in control and can help ourselves and others, every day.

Contents

Morning:
Strong as a Tree

*P*lace your feet on the floor.
In your mind's eye, see how you have tree roots underneath your feet, beautifully connected with Mother Earth.

*A*s you breathe in, the tree energy, bathed with light, enters your legs.
On the next breath in, the energy moves higher, into your belly and chest.
On the next breath in, the energy fills your back, arms, hands, and shoulders.
On the next breath in, let your neck and head and all around you be filled with the tree's energy.

*Y*ou feel strong and happy! End by saying, "Thank you for this fabulous new day!"

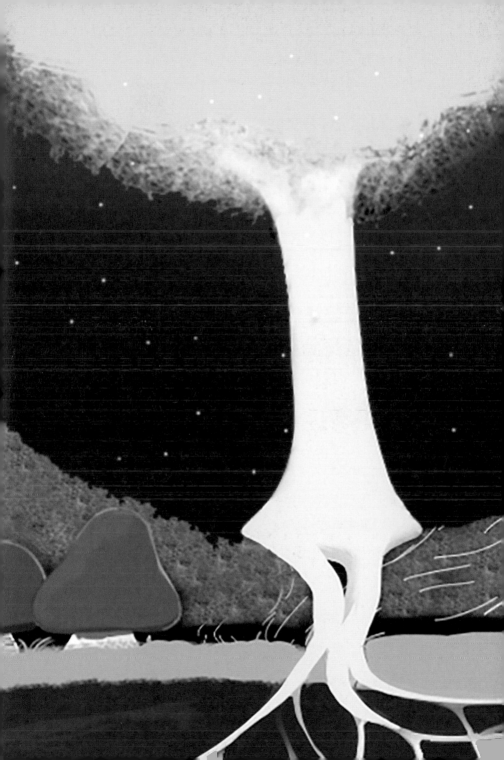

Self-Value:
Ladybirds

Sit comfortably. You may want to close your eyes, breathe calmly, and relax.

Imagine sitting in a big field of grass. It is a beautiful day. The sun is shining, and the wind is blowing softly.

You might want to briefly think of those "I can't do it" moments that are hanging around you. They look dark and sad.

Imagine now that there are little red ladybirds in the grass. Notice how those gentle and kind little red bugs crawl up and around you. Notice how they fly towards those unkind words and sad feelings.

Imagine the little red ladybirds eating the unpleasant words, thoughts, or actions of other people, or those you direct towards yourself.

As the bugs eat these words and actions, you feel better and better and better. Everything around you lightens up.

Don't worry, it doesn't harm the little creatures. They are part of our magic nature and will make those energies disappear easily.

You can do anything.

When you are ready,
you might want
to wriggle your toes and fingers.

Open your eyes.

Illness / Pain:
Healing Fairy Dust

*I*magine that fairies sprinkle gold healing glitter all over and around you.

Now imagine that the golden glitter is being fully absorbed into your body, especially in the places where you feel it's a bit dark or it hurts.

*I*f you really don't feel well enough, ask your mum or dad or someone you trust and who cares for you to imagine this healing for you.

Feel how, where it is darker in your body, where it hurts, the magic golden dust makes it melt and instead of dark, it now becomes light, which means it is healthy.

When you feel ready, open your eyes.

*T*rust

Unsettled:
Nature Awareness

Go out into nature, or
imagine being there.
Breathe in and out calmly.
Feel the grass and the wind on
your skin.
Hear the birds and the bees
singing and buzzing.
Smell the air and breathe it in
deeply.
Everything is fine.

Hug your dog. Feel the texture of his fur. Feel his sloppy kisses, which make you laugh.

Stroke your cat. Feel how she tickles your nose with her tail, which makes you smile.

You might want to walk through your garden, noticing the colours and smell the flowers. Smelling like a peach? An apple? A strawberry? Or maybe some smelly ones!

A fox or deer might just run through the garden and make you stand with wonder.

Keep that feeling, as it feels so nice, and get on with your fabulous day you have now created.

Tired:
"Powerful Yellow"

*E*very colour makes you feel a certain way.

When you are tired, use yellow.

Look at what is yellow, the sun!

Close your eyes, and breathe in and out to relax.

Allow your attention to go to your stomach.

Imagine a big sun in your body. It shines so bright you need sunglasses.

Every time you breathe in, the sun gets bigger.

Feel the excitement and happiness!

After a few breaths, open your eyes.

Fear
Archangel Michael

Imagine seeing Archangel Michael.

He glows with purple light and has a friendly smile.

Imagine feeling his energy.

He makes you feel safe and happy.

You might want to fall asleep snuggled up in his beautiful white wings.

Talk to him in your mind. You can ask him anything.

Wait for his answer, as it always comes.

What do you feel?
What do you think?
What do you see?

His presence relaxes you.

It makes you know that everything will always be okay.

Exams/Competition
Let's Visualize

*C*lose your eyes, breathe, and relax.

Picture yourself experiencing the
outcome you want.

Where are you?
Is someone with you?
How do you feel?
Make sure it feels the best!

On your next breath out,
let your desired outcome go into space.
The Universe will make it perfect
and bring it to you in perfect time.

Keeping that feeling of excitement,
open your eyes.

Sad: Mother Earth Can Help

Make yourself comfortable on your knees in the grass, real or imaginary.

Place your knees, hands, and forehead on the grass. Lean back with your bum on your calves, and relax.

Imagine the sad energy being sucked down into Mother Earth, away from you.

It comes out of your knees, hands, and forehead.

You can see this energy in a colour or a form.

Maybe you see rocks, slime or snakes coming out?

Whatever you see is fine, as long as you see this sad energy leaving your body and going into Mother Earth.

When that's done, feel how Mother Earth kisses you full of happiness. It tickles and feels lovely.

Open your eyes.

Trepidation/Insecurity
Breathing in Colours

Breathe in the colour red and feel strong,
safe, and powerful!
Say: *"I am allowed to be."*

Breathe in the colour orange to feel warm,
creative, and happy.
Say: *"I am allowed to feel."*

Breathe in the colour yellow, and feel energetic,
awake, and confident.
Say: *"I am allowed to show the world who I am."*

Breathe in the beautiful colour green,
and feel the love!
Say: *"I am allowed to love and to be loved."*

Breathe in the colour blue, and feel
comfortable in communicating. Say:
"I am allowed to hear and speak the truth."

Breathe in the deep warm purple, and
see all the beauty in the world!
Say: *"I am allowed to see."*

Breathe in pure white light and see it all around
you, making you know how special you are.
Say: *"I am special."*

YOU ARE
SO
SPECIAL

THANK YOU

THANK YOU

THANK YOU

THANK YOU

THANK

THANK YOU

THANK YOU

Gratitude:
Creating Lots of Happy Things

Every day, say thank you with all your heart
for at least five things!
Thank you for this food that nourishes my body.
Thank you for my bed, so I can safely snuggle up
and have a good night's sleep.
Thank you for this pen, so I can write things down.
Thank you for my arms, so I can hug my loved ones.
Thank you for this tree, which makes it possible
for me to breathe in clean air.

Take your time,
and say "thank you"
in your mind now.

It feels fantastic to say
"thank you!"

Protect your Energy
Favourite Coloured Light Bubble

At the beginning of your day, imagine standing inside a big balloon.

Fill your balloon with your favourite colour, whatever that may be!

It might be different every day.

*I*n this way, you can stand inside your happy energy.

Your good energy can go into the world to help and influence others positively.

The low, sad, uncomfortable, or angry energy of others will bounce off your balloon's surface, so it cannot affect you as much.

You are now ready for your day!

Busy Day Around Many People:
Cleansing Shower

*C*lose your eyes and imagine having a shower (or really go and have one).

See how the water washes all the dirt awa

Where it first seemed dark, it is now becoming brighter and lighter and you feel bett and better.

The dirt washes off you,
down the drain.

Turn your shower off,
and feel vibrant.
Relax.

Nervous / *Stress*
shhh

When baby cries and Mummy says *ssshh* in a soothing, sweet voice, baby quiets down.

When we feel stressed, and we feel like blowing up or running away, we need to quiet down that baby inside us.

Close your eyes and say *sssshhhhh, sssshhhh, ssshhh, shhh…* until you feel calmer and are now able to listen to your wise and calm self.

shhh

shhh

shhh

Fights
Restore the Balance

*C*lose your eyes, and breathe in and out a few times.

Say your friend's name in your mind or out loud.

Imagine seeing him or her standing in front of you.

Feel the anger that fight or situation made you feel,

Let it come up fully, then . . . whoosh . . . release it, throw it, blow it back to the other person.

If any energy from you is still with him or her, let that now come back to you.

Say:

"You are free. I am free. We are both free."

See how your friend turns around and walks away. When he is fully gone, open your eyes.

Anger
Crazy Runaround and Vacuum

Go outside, somewhere safe where there is space, and run, scream, shake your arms and legs.

Let it all out, for as long as needed!

Stand still.

Notice the angels placing a big vacuum cleaner above your head.

Turn it on with your imagination, and let the vacuum suck away all the anger left around you.

Drink a glass of water to cleanse.

Self-Love:
Notice Yourself

Massage your feet. Feel them; they carry your body, every day.

Massage your legs. They walk you everywhere, every day.

Appreciate your back. It keeps you strong and proud, every day.

Give yourself a tickle on the belly: laughing is so much fun!

Massage your shoulders. They deserve 'well done taps' from you every day.

Massage your arms and hands. They do all your carrying, handling, hugging, and giving and deserve to receive your attention every day.

Massage your head. It is in complete control of your beautiful life every day.

Say:

I love you "[your name]"

Trust
Breathe

*L*ay your hands on your belly.
Close your eyes and bring your
attention to your belly.
As you breathe in, your belly goes up.
As you breathe out, your belly goes down.

Breathe in, 2, 3
Breathe out, 2, 3
Breathe in, 2, 3
Breathe out, 2, 3
Breathe in, 2, 3
Breathe out, 2, 3
…

Everything will always be okay.

Loss:
We are all connected

Close your eyes and breathe to relax.

Say the name of the person you are missing, either in your mind or out loud.

In your mind's eye, see them standing in front of you.

Notice how they look.

Listen and watch. Maybe they have something to say.

Feel how you feel.

You can talk to them, too.

When you feel better, say, "Goodbye. See you next time."

Breathe in and out a bit deeper.

Wriggle your toes, move your hands, and open your eyes.

Unknown Territory:
My Friend the Dragon

Your dragon is next to you right now!

He is big but oh so kind.

What colour is he?

Has he got a long neck or tail?

Has he got wings?

He roars and blows out fire to protect you.

Snuggle up close to him. He is lovely and warm.

He stays awake all night and day, just to look after you.

So stand up tall and feel strong;
your dragon is with you,
always.

WORRY:

Emptying the Backpack of Worry

Close your eyes and breathe until you feel calm.

Notice the heavy weight of your worry backpack.

It pulls on your shoulders.

Imagine taking that backpack off.

You give it to the angels, who fly away with it until you can no longer see it.

"Thank you
angels!"

Helping Others:
Magic Fairy Wand

*W*ish others well!

Say in your mind:

"Thank you for his health."
Imagine him healthy.

"Thank you for his happiness."
Imagine seeing him smiling away,
happy with his life.

"Thank you for her wealth."
Imagine her with all the money she
needs and wants.

Good wishes send out so much
beautiful energy and always return.

Your Wishes Come True
Dream Your Dreams

*I*f you can dream it, you can achieve it.

You might want to close your eyes
and breathe in and out deeply until you
feel relaxed.

Imagine what you wish for.
See where you want it to be.
See who is there.
See precisely how you want it to be
and feel it.

Now take a deep breath in and when
you breathe out, give your dream to the
angels.

Now trust. It is yours!

FINDHORN PRESS

Life-Changing Books

Consult our catalogue online
(with secure order facility) on
www.findhornpress.com

For information on the Findhorn Foundation:
www.findhorn.org

Published by Findhorn Press
Text © Marie Delanote 2017 • Illustrations © Johannes Vandierendonck 2017
Edited by Nicky Leach • Interior design by Johannes Vandierendonck and Thierry Bogliolo
ISBN 978-1-84409-721-0
Printed and bound in the European Union